The
Book
of
Jade

The
Book
of
Jade

Yun Wang

Story Line Press
Ashland, Oregon

Published by Story Line Press, Three Oaks Farm, PO Box 1240,
Ashland, OR 97520-0055, www.storylinepress.com.

This publication was made possible thanks in part to the generous
support of the Nicholas Roerich Museum and our individual
contributors.

Cover design by Lysa McDowell
Interior design by Sharon McCann
Author photo by shevaunwilliams.com

Library of Congress Cataloging-in-Publication Data

Wang, Yun, 1964–
        The book of jade : poems / by Yun Wang.
            p. cm.

        ISBN 1-58654-023-8

    1. Chinese Americans—Poetry. 2. China—Poetry. I. Title.
    PS3623.A46 B66 2002
    811'.6—dc21
                                                    2002007755

For Tian

ACKNOWLEDGMENTS

Grateful acknowledgment goes to the following periodicals in which
these poems, sometimes in earlier versions, first appeared:
The Connecticut Poetry Review: "Once in a Train";
Green Mountains Review: "Beneath the Painted Shrine," "Jealousy,"
and "The Buffalo Man";
International Poetry Review: "Reading Mud in the Outhouse,"
"Threshold," and "The Small Mermaid";
International Quarterly: "Elegy for the Piano";
The Kenyon Review: "The Pain Fish";
The Pennsylvania Review: "April, White Blossoms" and
"Without Fear";
Poet Lore: "Crab Apple" (as "A Tree in Cultural Revolution");
Webster Review: "Loss in Spring."

Acknowledgment is also due to the following anthologies:
PREMONITIONS: The Kaya Anthology of New Asian American Poetry
(Kaya Production, 1994): "The Carp," "Beyond Hunger," and "Prisoner
of Mountains";
Multi-cultural Resources for English Teachers (Simon & Schuster,
1996): "The Carp."

The following poems appeared in the chapbook *The Carp* (Bull Thistle
Press, 1994):
"Childhood in China," "The Fair," "Loss in Spring," "Jealousy," "The
Yellow Books," "Beneath the Painted Shrine," "The Buffalo Man,"
"Beyond Hunger," "The Carp," "Crab Apple," "Prisoner of Mountains,"
and "Image from the Back" (as a postcard).

I thank Janet McAdams, Lara Candland and Julie Gozan for helpful
comments on a draft of the manuscript.

Contents

VIII. Once in a Train

IX. The Book of Tian

Notes

I

The Book of Mirrors

*For my father, Wang Zhengchu
and my mother, Li Meiying*

He Would Not Bow Down His Head

Aunt says his head was damaged. Father tells the same stories many times.

He held his head high before the Red Guards. They beat him with iron bars. They kicked his unconscious body all over the big stage, where others kneeled with lowered eyes. Ten thousand spectators shouted slogans.

I was obsessed with orchids. The early spring wind smooth as water.

"When the blood-thirsty Japanese came," Father would recite, as he led me and my sister upon the mountain. "I was made Commander of Local Resistance, at age sixteen!" Father raised his voice. My sister turned to me, winking.

A strand of unearthly fragrance drifted in the air.
In the greenness of the mountain, Father's snowy hair floated.

A Metaphor For the Sage,
After Qu Yuan

A slender green orchid
A young maiden lingering
by clear streams upon the mountain

Leopards and tigers pulled her chariot
all the way from her dwelling
deep in bamboo forests

The rain brought dusk
The green scent deepened
Her tears and the blackness of her hair
wove into the night

Monkeys gibbered
Apes chattered
The prince did not come

Dissecting the Orchids

In its mimicry, the orchid adapts whatever trait is most appealing to the pollinator. One orchid generates an aromatic oil that the males of a particular species of bees need, desperately, if they are to woo females.

Some orchids look and smell like female bees, irresistible decoys to the males. Some have the odor of rotting meat, coaxing any nearby carrion beetles to come hither.

Wrinkled bulbs grow at the orchid stem's base.
The Greeks named the entire plant after their word for testicle.

The orchids are rare flowers, cannot afford to waste nectar on an insect likely to rummage around for any old sweetness, and drop pollen at any site.

Chang-e Drank the Potion of Immortality

The Imperial Mother of Gods and Goddesses had given Chang-e's husband the potion of immortality as a reward.

Her husband was the big hero who shot down nine suns, thus saving the earth from being charred.

Some say Chang-e did it by mistake. Others say it was out of curiosity, or greed.

Chang-e drank up the whole thing, was uprooted into the air. She rose and rose, all the way to the moon.

There she is, weeping, in those shadows that are osmanthus trees. There is no one else there, except a celestial man exiled for theft by the court of the immortals. His punishment has been to cut down the osmanthus trees that instantly grow back, as they fall under his ax.

All versions agree on her beauty.

The Missing Eye

I do not have my mother's eyes. She lost one of them. They took it out, but there was no cancer.

"You should be proud of yourself," my father said, "for having stayed in one of the hospitals that admit only the high officials."

The moon was a golden melon. Darkness welled up in me.
I could not look at my mother.

I do not have my father's eyes. His are Manchu eyes. We are not Manchu. My eyes have the shape of willow leaves.

The moon was in the mouth of darkness. There was a little star close to the moon. "You are the flesh of my heart," my mother whispered.

The Eagle Has Landed

"That's one small step for man, one giant leap for mankind," said the astronaut. The whole world watched him, heard his words. Except for those who had neither radio nor TV.

The moon was revealed to the civilized world as a lifeless place. One side farther below freezing than you can imagine.

There is no air or water. Only the huge blue Earth in the sky.

The Buddhist Master Chose His Successor

On the highest mountain, monks lined up in the temple. The
head disciple chanted:

> My body is erect as a lime-tree
> My heart clear as a bright mirror
> Oft would I tend my mind
> Let not the dust taint it

Applause from the round of other clean-robed disciples.

The cook overheard, shouted from the kitchen:

> The lime-tree is no tree
> The mirror is not there
> All are names nothing exists
> Whence does dust descend?

The Master opened his eyes, nodded.

The Eyes of the Beggar

We ate turnips and rice for meals. We had surprise visits from old men in rags. They had long dry voices, would sometimes get down on their knees.

I was frightened by them, would run to shut the door. Then the persistent banging of a fist. My mother would go to give them rice, then scold me for being heartless.

I could never look into the eyes of beggars. Except those of this blind one, who sat still on the iron bridge. He bowed slowly on two-stringed er-hu. His eyes were peaceful mirrors. Passers-by chatted with him, taunted him for stories.

"Once, a lady who ran away from home wanted to join me. Can you imagine," he said. "I told her, come on closer so I can feel between your thighs." The adults roared in laughter. They said, "You are sick."

According to a Leading Cosmologist

There are different solutions: to hide the dirt under the rug, or to push it out of one's house. Different people study the Universe, using different coordinate systems.

If God knew theoretical physics, he would not have attempted to create the Universe.

Consider this cartoon of drunken sailors: one sailor sees the bottle to the right of himself, another sailor sees it to the left of himself. Hence the bottle cannot be real. However, there is definitely something real inside the bottle.

If God could work alone, he would create a perfectly homogeneous Universe which would expand, then collapse.

Due to the devil's destructive work, the Universe resembles not a single balloon, but a permanently growing tree, consisting of many large bubbles, connected to each other.

God inflates the Universe. The devil drills a hole into it.

II

Loss in Spring

Childhood in China

Hui's Grandma tied silk flowers in her braids.
My hair was cut short after they found lice.

I never saw my grandparents.
Mother was abandoned at age three.
Father's parents died long ago,
leaving their children to be punished
for owning land before Liberation.

The mountains were forever green. In rice fields, waves of
pointed hats with huge rims. Trouser-legs rolled above the
calves, people planted seedlings deep in the mud. I screamed:
a leech clung to my leg.

Hui was not afraid of crawling things,
says she resembled a worm at birth.

Hui's Grandpa seemed not to have noticed her. After his death,
they found a note recording the horoscope of her birth under his
pillow. She wore a white robe, performed kowtow in his funeral
procession.

I have dreamed about my grandparents.
The paternal ones had a vast pond.
Double stemmed lotus. Golden carps leaping.
The maternal ones have not appeared.
Mother whispers different versions at different times.

The Fair

Tomatoes, onions, wild mushrooms. Chickens and eggs, sweet
potatoes. Against iron railings peasants sat, guarding their goods
with narrowed eyes. Sun-dried hot peppers, sacks of tea leaves.
Jasmine flowers opening in the sun.

The river drowned in shadows. The bridge, a river of people
ebbing and flowing, disrupted: someone snatched a chicken and
ran. The gray-haired peasant woman wailed for the last chicken
from her yard.

The town policeman caught the little thief, took off his belt
before the shivering boy, whose drunkard father watched.
The thick belt flew, a wind of knives.

A crowd gathered around the beating, cheering.
The old peasant woman pushed through, begged the policeman
to stop.

Mother bought the chicken from the old woman for more than
she asked for. She reminded Mother of our babysitter who
ground grains and fed chickens, leaving me and my sister in the
mud to play, the same way she brought up her own.

Loss in Spring

Around us, azaleas in furious bloom:
white, fuchsia, scarlet.

Shan knelt, waved the sickle. The strong scent of green juice
surged. Spinach weeds for pigs, fenced in behind her family's
outhouse. I cut a few leaves carefully, then plucked azaleas.

Against the sapphire sky, upon the jade slope,
the clusters formed luminous clouds.

Shan stopped work to help me. We sat, laps full of azaleas.
She handed me a red stem, "Eat this, it's sweet. Best ones bloom
on wild tombs." She pointed to a small mound: crimson azaleas
burst out of cogongrass tall as us.

Shan told me her father had dreamed of people digging a hole in
the ground. He asked what they were doing. "Planting some
flowers," they said. Shan's mother died a week later.

The stem slipped from my fingers,
red as blood, fell upon the earth.

The mountain wind moistened with Shan's voice. "Will you still
remember me someday, gathering flowers in your garden?"

Jealousy

My mother had this repetitive dream:
my sister and I, a pair of white lotus flowers
washed by black currents
to opposite directions.

*Once there were two sisters named First Orchid and Second
Orchid, who washed clothes together by the river. First Orchid
was pushed into the water, sank without a trace.*

Everyone loved my sister, who laughed and ran
waving her little arms imitating Red Guards.
She sat in Aunt's lap near the fire.
I hid in the corner reading pasted newspapers
turning yellow on the wall.

*First Orchid returned in silk and gold to her shocked sister, told
the story of the giant serpent. How he swept her into his under-
water palace. How he turned into a man at night and lay
beside her.*

Father visited from the reform camp,
asked me to recite poems by Li Bai.
My sister shrieked, made faces to me.
When she fell asleep by my side that night,
I dug my thumb into my nose then wiped it
on my sister's broad forehead.

*Second Orchid cried about her patched clothes. Her sister
exchanged clothes with her. When they reached the river,
Second Orchid jumped into the water and drowned.*

My sister leaped up in bed, grabbed my hair.
Her screams brought a bamboo whip
and Aunt's voice, a knife scrubbing
on a stone: "You retarded brat,
you evil-hearted wolf."

The Yellow Books

Only children watched the burning. My friends poked the fire
with sticks, warned me not to peek into such books. I caught
half-singed pages flying about with the ashes:

> *Tanya bathes in the river, her body blooming
> in its pureness... Paul watches, his heart
> aches... Suddenly a beastly laugh... The soldier
> chases her while shedding his clothes... Paul
> jumps out from the bushes and knocks the Tsar's
> soldier into the river...*

* * *

Mrs. Deng's bright-eyed daughter walked funny, lifting one foot
only. Mrs. Deng's son was in prison, for counter-revolutionary
speeches and reading "yellow books." Hundreds were found
when the town policeman searched their home.

It was whispered that one day a peasant went to the town police
station. Someone had stolen his goat. He saw the policeman on
top of his tearful daughter, her mouth stuffed with cloth. The
peasant's family background was investigated.

Before Mrs. Deng's son was executed, his lame sister went to
see him.

III

The Book of Windows

Passengers

We wake up one morning,
find ourselves on the train.

Not a single day passes without us
witnessing someone
crushed by the wheels.
Sometimes they seem to be people
identical to ourselves.
There is no explanation how anyone
could have gotten off the train.
It never stops.

We have never seen the driver.
Men in long white robes
push carts filled with blue glass bottles
toward the front of the train.

We reach our palms
out of narrow slits in the windows
to gather rain water and snow.
We drink to the pale lips
of moonlight, purple trumpets
of morning glories, yellow trumpets
of daylilies.

We speculate and postulate
on the destination of the train.
Our primeval curiosity
fuels the train.

Space

The windows of space are not
the stars
They are the darkness in between

The Driver

Too many sunsets.
Various ways of shearing the light.
Two swans drift on darkening shadows.
What is the point?

Spring is holding out,
hides her slender fingers in parched branches,
covers her face with a veil of dull gray.
Mystery is renewed.
The same old Spring
will hawk the same flowers
with slightly different faces.
Very few would notice.

And the swans,
if you build a bridge in the woods
they will crash into it and break their long necks.
Too late to turn by the time they see it.
You must paint the bridge Yellow.

The Choice

She charted the land of inscribed caves. He waited for her in one of them.

The merchants kidnapped her, brought her to Him in ropes.

She saw Him sitting by a giant statue of herself. He ordered her untied. He recounted their ancient oath of love, begged her to step through a fire of diamond and sapphire, to become immortal again.

A voice whispered in her ear: "This is only a movie, now is the time for you to topple the statue and run."
She has heard this voice too many times.
She walked into the fire.

Goddess With a Shovel

Men thought ghosts in dark woods
made women pregnant.
They worshiped Her, feared Her.

When they made the connection
between semen and conception,
they burned down Her temple.

They enslaved women,
sold them as merchandise.
They used women as birthing machines.

She returned with a shovel.
Where She dug, roses bloomed:
red as blood shed in childbirth,
thorny as inescapable love.

The Parable of Love

A man traps a bird.
He complains of her sad, listless notes.
She wraps herself in her blue wings.

She appears dead.
He buries her in a glossy white box.

He drives a car at night
with the lights off.
He climbs into the white box
to ask her one more question.

The Willow Dream

Each time it rains the hollows fill with water. The willow trees confront distorted faces of themselves.

The sky blinds me with such blue, as I have not seen since I looked into your cold, amused eyes. You considered my breasts. If I had given a small sign, your thin fingers would have landed there. Slender willow leaves drifting on water.

I can not hold myself responsible for your lack of sufficient interest.

I put my arms around your brother, his warm lips caress my thoughts to sleep. In the deserted shipyard he towers over me. His thrusts ring in my ears and echo off ships which will travel to the four seas, after being laboriously mended.

Your twin sister recites The Odyssey in ancient Greek, tilting her head ever so slightly. The sun paints her exquisite silhouette in the water, brimming with drunken blue of the sky. I drown myself beneath her shadow. She looks down and is startled by willow leaves turning scarlet.

A Harvesting

Darkness fills bare stalks of rice plants.
I tread the thorny matrices
in search of a single stem laden with grains.

A dark stranger hooded in black
raises his orange lantern.
He has finally found me:
small, barefoot, shivering in rags.
I am no longer afraid of his face.
He gazes into my eyes from holes
nested in bleached bones.

When I wake I find myself lying
flat and motionless
on a black-lacquered table
surrounded by people of my own blood.
They slice me with rusted knives.
They drain my blood into a Ming vase.
They are hungry.
Father, Sisters, Aunt, Cousins.
And others I have never met.
They put me into white porcelain bowls
rimmed with tiny crimson roses.
They raise their cow-bone chopsticks.

Somewhere, Mother's voice,
a hay in the needle stack:
"No, we can not do this to her."

Rising

I speed to the edge of the cliff
My wings open
I am in the air

The green of the mountains recedes
The blue of the sky fades
over my naked limbs

IV

Beneath the Painted Shrine

Beneath the Painted Shrine

Furious waves of incense and Ming's voice
echoing: "Marry me."
When she refused he rode off
to join the People's Liberation Army.

In ancient times there was a woman
who leaped into the burning furnace
when her husband failed to forge the sword
that the emperor desired.

Father coughs in the next room.
Mother begins to snore in the carved chair.
She rises from the floor, steps outside
the back door. Rain water streams off bamboo
splashes on two black coffins
stacked against the wall.

She holds out a hand
into the rain, recalls his hand holding hers
to help her practice calligraphy.

At home a woman obeys her parents,
after marriage her husband,
after husband's death her son.
Confucius has been quoted for thousands of years.
She imagines Ming in his green uniform
leafing through a thread-bound book.

The husband made the perfect sword
in the fire his wife had become.
The emperor was pleased.

The Buffalo Man

At the bottom of Night she shivers
in her underwear. Over her the unmoving stars:
eyes of dead fish.
The town policeman behind his closed door
told her to go home and have no fear.
Leaping off the bed with a bleeding forehead,
she had run away
from her roaring husband.

Two years ago falling petals
of peach blossoms colored the wind.
He took her to his house
for an evening cup of tea.
The scent of jasmine rose and faded.
She tried to push him off but his mother
had locked the door from outside.
She married, bore him a son
three months after the wedding.

Night sprawls over her, streets pushing her
from each side. This has happened before.
Once upon a time there was a woman named Lotus
whose husband beat her, kicked her out of the house.
She dared to contradict his mother
who gave orders from a carved chair.
Lotus sat by the well for three days and nights,
did not jump in. She pulled up the bucket.
There was a frog inside.

She returns home to an empty house.
Her clothes, cut into ribbons.
Inside the mirror the blood-stained pale face
nested in tangles of black hair.

She climbs the hill at dawn,
her clothes smelling of moth-balls.
Purple sun glow drapes over the grave
of her mother. She kneels.

Eyes closed, she feels Mother's warm fingers
combing and braiding her hair
in a curtained corner of Father's clay hut.
Rain water dripped
from the ceiling into barrels on the floor.

Her breasts swell with milk.
She recalls Father's bad-tempered buffalo
who knocked her over when she guided him.
Her knees bled but he ploughed the field willingly.
The frog turned into a good man for Lotus,
built a house for her, gave her sons.
She plucks herbs to cover her forehead
starts downhill, to look for her child.

Beyond Hunger

The little girl returned empty handed.
Corpses lay bloated in sunset fields.
Not a leaf on the trees, not a grass root left.
She opened the door of the hut and saw
steam rising from the wok, her father
sitting in the corner eating.

Far away in a room with plush green carpets
Mao put down a thread-bound book,
walked to his desk, unrolled silken white
paper, dipped the writing-brush in ink:
Snow dances like silver dragons
Horsemen and torches on the Great Wall
Mighty Genghis Khan pulls back the bow
shoots down a giant eagle

The little girl ran out screaming the name
of her baby brother. Night dropped its shroud.
She searched until she collapsed
in an empty warehouse.
Her stomach muttered, then no sound.
A gentle mist came, almost a fragrance.

She could see the fields in another spring.
She sang, gathering dandelions.
Her baby brother ran after grasshoppers.

It was sunny that day in Beijing.
Mao gave a speech on the evil intent of rumors
of starvation.
Afterwards he put on a straw hat,
visited a model kindergarten.
The roses drooped a little in the courtyard.
Mao posed for pictures with the children
who smiled like spring flowers and Tomorrow
as he told them they were.

The little girl was angry at her baby brother
who put a grasshopper in his mouth.
Just then it thundered.
The lightning blinded her, she started.
The door opened, light poured in
above a shadow, upon a butcher knife.
She heard herself saying: *Please don't Father*
Who will take care of you when you are old

Elegy for the Piano

I. Irreversible Journey

An almost empty train
passing dead chimneys, tunnels, trains
full of Red Guards going the opposite way
to Beijing, where he stood before her
at the train station, his eyes blazing,
his luggage at his feet, his father's bodyguard
nudging his elbow, urging him to go home.

Alone she rode the train through three nights.
When she got off, an old man in patched clothes
greeted her against a backdrop of hay stacks.
After a pine forest and crossing creeks
on single logs, she was shown
a gathering of clay huts
in the mouth of a deep valley.

Look at those hands, the peasants sighed.
You can tell she has never used them.
The village girls giggled, pointed at her covering
her mouth with a handkerchief.
They dipped barrels into a pond of excrement.
She bent with her right shoulder beneath the bar,
tried to stand up but the barrels were too full.

Leaving rape fields at dusk, she looked up.
The constellations: diamonds on dark
velvet, a dress she once wore
to play Chopin before the vaulted window.
It opened into a garden of white roses.
Before they burned the books, smashed the piano.
Before his father, a factory worker, became
the governor, and her parents who were professors
drank pesticide.

II. Mud

A lamb goes to the creek.
A wolf is there.
He approaches her with fangs showing,
tells her that the creek is his,
she must pay for drinking his water.
The lamb can do nothing.
The wolf needs no excuse.

The odor of field fertilizers surged.
Mud splashed, new grass died beneath her.
Pain and fear tore her with razor teeth.
She felt herself buried alive
deeper into the mud
with each fall of his weight.

Scars on his face, his breath
scourging her face.
She could not take her eyes off
the knife in his pocket.

The sky distanced itself
pulling the light with it.

She knew that screams would reach no one.
He was the village Party leader.
The peasants left her behind in haste,
urged buffalos with bamboo whips.
In their huts over the hills
they lit oil-lamps behind bolted doors.

III. The Return

She took the train back to the city, walked down streets lined
with bullet-holed buildings. The reward from the man who raped
her.

The sun came down in furious waves. A sensation of drowning.
Piano notes surfaced in her mind. She watched the smooth
current of bicycles. Someone got off his bicycle, walked toward
her. She knew it was the governor's son, who had wanted to
follow her to the end of the world.

It amazed her that he simply asked for her handkerchief, spoke
so softly she almost did not hear him. She saw herself in his deep
gaze. A white rose spoiled by worms. He got on his bicycle,
glided away, before her lips could move.

She turned around the corner, saw a poster on the notice board.
It announced the death of the governor's son, dated three
months ago.

Following plum trees with white blossoms, she found his tomb.
She knew it was his, because her handkerchief, white with green
orchids, lay on the mound, carefully spread out. Her fingers
burned as they lifted the handkerchief. Beneath it, a note: *You
have profaned our love.*

She awoke to blank walls of the hospital. A friend of his, an
actor, carried her there from the cemetery. She refused food and
explanations, died three months pregnant.

Image from the Back

At dawn the heads of those
who sought to free the people
fall under crescent knives sharpened
beneath painted eaves

The mother sits day and night by the river
IIer reflection lost in muddy ripples
Her hair gathered into a black fist

What is the meaning of sacrifice

A peddler wanders deep streets
attracting crowds of vacant faces
He sells good-luck bread soaked
fresh in the martyrs' blood

V

The Book of Scarlet

For Susan and Scarlet Sheppard

Susan's Cat

When light is withdrawn from the sky
it is shut within the cat's eyes

His black fur shapes the air
His pupils grow into round lamps

The cat hears

A rustle of faded silk
A body ten thousand miles away
across the ocean and beneath mountains
in a shroud woven of gold medallions

In the cradle the baby sleeps
Her breath a fresh sweetness

The cat ponders in the dark
It has licked the baby's head all over
brushed the hair on her forehead
into seven black columns

The Perfect Hand

Having created paintings that conquered the world, the old man withdrew. It was said that he wished to reach the final perfection in secrecy.

A dashing young painter had a sea-green eyed beloved, his model, fragile as porcelain. He offered her to the old man.

After three months, the young man learned of his beloved's death. He was allowed into the studio. Holding his breath, he lifted one corner of the red velvet curtain. He saw a hand beautiful beyond description.

The young painter closed his eyes. He threw open the thick curtain. There, the canvas blazed in whiteness of indistinguishable layers of paint.

Written in Stars

A great wall stretches
three hundred million lightyears
We are not certain of its existence

The black mirrors are embroidered
They speak to us in waves
As we breathe our thoughts are read
A cold sensation

These faint blossoms emerge
out of darkness
As we gaze they grow brighter

In the celestial ocean of dust
there are lumps that glow
there are lumps that are dark
there are voids that grow

The Orphaned Martian

A man walks through streets of night.
He feels that he is being followed.
There is no sound.
He dares not turn his head.

O lend me the right voice
so that you may love me.

The man has not seen this dog before.
The man is a lonely student from China.
He looks at the dog, becomes puzzled.

O lend me the right shape
so that I may be safe.

The man sighs, closes the door,
opens the door again.
Feeding the dog, the man wonders
what he should do tomorrow.

Helen of the Hinterland

"Look," she pointed to herself, "This is a face that can launch
a thousand ships."

Helen was not drunk. She had just spent a night in jail for
drunken driving. Steam and smoke mingled into abstract
landscapes inside the half-lit bar.

Her friend, a beautiful woman, was unnerved by the gazes of
men with hungry looks. "Have you noticed how they stare at
me," said Helen.

Helen had two children by the same married man.
The first was an accident. The second, to trick him.

Sitting cross-legged, Helen blew a mouthful of smoke in her
friend's face.

There Is No Escape

Wherever we are
the Universe
is bound
to collapse
Either we are
in a dense region
a black hole
is imminent
Or on a
grand scale
we are
enclosed
within
a heavy shell

The Baby shall have
no evidence
we ever
existed
We can contrive
to make the baby
so strange
those
who come to be
in the New
Universe
will be
compelled to
speculations

By making a Baby Universe
we can save part of ourselves

A Foreign Language

Down the corridor of many opened doors
came a glowing white apparition.
I could see although I closed my eyes
so tight that tears welled up.

I was twelve, with short black hair.
Outside the house, yellow daylilies
that would only open at night.
Their fragrance suffocated.

A cry was choking me. The white figure
stopped half way, disappeared.
I decided to grow my hair very long
and learn a very foreign language.

I imagined words that turn to wild grass
after one has looked long enough.
Their sounds would persist in my ears
stringing and bending many thoughts.

A Man Said:

I have found you very inspiring.
Did you notice me sort of
avoiding you at Hemingway's?

Had to distance myself
to find my balance.

What's that noise?
Is it your phone or mine?
Hope it's not mine.

The other night I had a scary dream
involving cannibalism.
I was disgusted.
When you walked over that night,
I was telling it to a colleague,
so he could diagnose it for me.

I don't think men could ever
find you repulsive.
Maybe some women could.

Anyway, don't be offended
if I avoid you.
I noticed you are becoming friends
with Susan, that's good.

Not Written in the Stars

There are rivers that are mirrors, reflecting green branches.
There are rivers that are scarlet, rushing beneath the skin.

The glowing end of incense fades instantly, falls.

The sun dances on the streams, her golden hair tangled in the
waves. Who is this darkness that cuts off her hair, wraps the
world in his opaque cloak?

Flowers, then petals, one by one in the cold wind.

There is nothing that can change the color of the warm river.
The moon spreads her silver veil when the mother calls out to
her child.

VI

Prisoner of Mountains

The Carp

My father was the school principal. The day I was born, he
caught a twenty pound carp. He gave it to the school kitchen.
All the teachers and boarding students tasted it.

Waves of mountains surrounded us. I grew up yearning for the
ocean. Smoke arose from green mountains to form clouds each
morning. My father named me Cloud.

When a son was born to Confucius, the king of Lu sent over a
carp as present. Confucius named his son Carp.

The wise say a carp leaping over the dragon gate is a very lucky
sign. My father says he named me Cloud because I was born in
the year of the dragon: there are always clouds following a
dragon. Confucius' son died an early death. My father has only
three daughters.

When I was three, I wandered all over the campus. A stray cat in
a haunted town. My mother says I passed the room where my
father was imprisoned. He whispered to me, hid a message
in my little pocket. It was his will that I should grow up a strong
woman, and find justice for him.

They caught me. My father was beaten to near death. Some of
them were students, whose parents were peasants. Some of them
were teachers, who used to be his best friends. They had tasted
the carp.

It has been recorded that Confucius could not tell the difference between millet and wheat, and was thus mocked by a peasant. This peasant became a big hero, representing the wisdom of the people, thousands of years after Confucius' death.

My father still goes fishing, the only thing that seems to calm him. The mountains are sleeping waves. My father catches very small fish. My mother eats them. My friends laugh at me, when I tell them that once upon a time, my father caught a carp weighing twenty pounds.

Reading Mud in the Outhouse

Limestone dust was strewn around the holes in the outhouse.
But the maggots wiggled unharmed, climbed near my shoes. I
would have died if the white-washed wall were not splashed by
mud: figures in fancy coiffures and ballet poses calmed me from
their casts of clean mud.

The mud fresco trained my eyes to see aliens shifting shapes in
passing clouds, according to what they thought.

A furnace worker was beaten to death for jesting about
compensations for Father, imprisoned for years because of his
diaries. In an over-lit street corner a town drunk hit Mother on
the eye for trying to stop him from beating a student. People
relished calling me retarded. Each sunset I sat by the river.

Many fish jumped into the sun for me. A silver firework that
signified the secret significance of my life.

Sometimes the army of darkness marched on the drumbeat of
one's heart. Father did not come home. Mother took to bed with
Meuniere's disease. I had nightmares, could not avoid going to
the outhouse. I gazed at the mud figures on the wall. Light
leaked in from the opening near the roof. I could not see their
faces but knew. They feared nothing, always held their places
with grace.

Threshold

Mother feared malice eyes. She walked with her back bent,
yielding to the weight of air. When she woke me in the morning,
her breath stung. Stems of forgotten irises in shallow water,
unchanged for weeks.

I grew up in fear of becoming Mother
drowning in shadows of gossip.
The insatiable fish fed on us.

Father's political scars. Mother's face aged in her early thirties.
The gossipers chewed with varying spices. Aunt befriended them
by distributing stories of me, so retarded that I failed to split a
coal block with a hammer. She brought home stories of other
children. How they revealed genius in mischief. How a girl
suddenly refused to eat fruits, the only way her mother
discovered: she had her first period.

I buried myself in books, pored over
peonies withering in the yard.
The gossipers snickered over my shoulders.

One night I felt a warm sticky current running down my thighs.
I cried for Mother, she brought stacks of pink tissue paper. Her
eyes soothed me with glow of dark sapphire. Her thin face
brimmed with soft light. I knew then, Mother was beautiful once.
"You will have babies one day," she whispered. The scarlet
fountain sent gentle shocks, relaxed me head to toe.

I began to look straight into the eyes
of gossipers, they startled and fled:
sparrows caught stealing grain.

Crab Apple

Before our door was this tree, low, heavy with white fragrance in spring. The school clerk's peasant wife chopped it down for fire-wood.

She needed a lot of fire-wood to cook for eight of her nine children. Her eldest son joined the People's Liberation Army. Her youngest was a half-wit, always drooling and peeing in the yard.

*   *   *

At wintertime the faucet in the yard dripped freezing water.
I had to wash vegetables, dirty dishes, my baby-sister's diapers.
I would shudder more when I saw the peasant's daughter come over with a bucket of something.

She made the whole class boo when I walked into the classroom. She taught me many lessons because I could not lie, because my father was a counterrevolutionary.

*   *   *

I missed the low tree with blossoms each spring, watching the peasant woman sit in the yard. Her wide face smiling in the sun, she picked lice out of the long hair of her daughter, who squatted, a proud and defiant princess.

I was not superstitious yet tears came to my eyes, when I saw many trees white with blossoms, on my long train ride away from home.

Prisoner of Mountains

Imagine people hating you so much
they spread tales of your death.
With sad faces they elaborate
how they brought your heart-broken parents
from the empty train station into their homes.

On the platform Father ran to me
his gray hair waving in the crowd
a worn banner in the mountain wind.

Barefoot children followed us.
Peeling posters draped the street in red.
Eyes tracked us from half closed windows.
Crying, Mother rose from the wicker chair,
her thin arms wrapped tightly around me.

Father and I wandered beneath pale stars
along paths through rice fields. Fireflies
flickered to the far barking of dogs.

"They never rest. How they loathe me
for telling the truth. They beat me senseless
with iron rods. They asked the Red Guards
to lock me up. They told everyone
you were retarded. My child,
how you have disappointed them."

In Father's youth, he climbed to mountain tops
with friends who wanted to design airplanes.
They drank and recited wild Li Bai.
They planned the future until the sun rose
and cast their blotted images
at the mountains' feet.

The Pain Fish

The only time Father cried out in pain
he lay in a hospital bed with three broken ribs.
Red Guards never made Father break his silence—
a hundred clubs striking left scars on his head.

Mother says he fell from the riverbank while fishing
on the winter solstice.
Mother weeps at his ingratitude.
He could not move for three months—
Mother fed and changed him.

Father says Mother is a little mouse who bites
those who are down and close but she trembles
near any scum of a person gloating over success.
He mocks how she would gobble tiny fish
and spit out all one hundred tiny bones.
He keeps fishing, supplies her with small fish.

We are defined by the blood we shed;
the blood on Mother's underpants smelled of rust
I washed it off in freezing winter in an enamel basin;
blood seeped through the door I closed
when Father cut a chicken's throat for Spring Festival;
a broken glass cut into my knee when I fell while running—
I was fascinated by the fine imprint in blood.

Father sits on the balcony making a fishnet,
behind him vermilion begonias in three clay pots.
Weaving nylon cords with a wooden guide,
Father whispers of his loneliness— how things
are decided behind him even in the family,
how he fell from the riverbank for a reason.

The Small Mermaid

Mother emptied chamber pots for wealthy classmates at her
boarding school. She grew up by the sea, can eat small fish like
no one else in the mountains: half a dozen into her mouth, out
come tiny bones.

Father goes fishing at dawn, returns in late sun.
A layer of small fish in the bamboo basket.

Mother tells how it feels to stand before the sea: the mind opens,
a folded sheet dropped in water. Dreams of swimming in that
small river at home, started years before I learned to swim, now
return with floods and dragon boats. Naked bodies shine among
small fish.

Mother cut my hair short each year for fear of lice. I screamed.

Now I will grow no taller. My hair rushes toward my feet.
Kneeling on a New Jersey beach littered with coke bottles and
potato-chip bags, I gaze into the sea bending over like Mother,
whose breath I avoided in mornings as a child.

Mother writes: "I feel with you."
Father writes: "Do not come home until my seventieth birthday."

A pimpled white man relates stories of the exotic toy shop in
Berkeley, where he bought a stick to use on his lower part. He
explains how it is to him, like life itself. I show him an enlarged
photo of a marble statue under the sea.

VII

The Book of Ebony

For Christopher K. Koenigsberg

The Earth Bleeds

There are holes into night
where bruises are engraved
where bodies are torn
limb from limb
There are no eyes to see
except those of the predator
who cuts his fellow species
into small pieces

He smiles

Grass blades lie still in dark heat
There are windows but they are closed
Sirens leap from silence
screaming toward him
They are snuffed out by his smile
There are no eyes to see
in the caves of the predator

To the Sky

Let us build temples that shall stand
till the last day of the last one of us
Let us have temples that house
what gods there may be

Temples are built also to be ruined
so that in times to come
the fixed stars shall locate the ruins
greater temples may be imagined

Let men carve giant stones
off mountains near the sky's edge
Let them set the stones on ships
cross hundreds of rivers
and bring them into the desert

An identical monument shall be erected
every one hundred years
Let strong arms be spent in labor
Let dark minds be drowned
by the pure white glaze
of these celestial mirrors

In the Streets

What do we know
that the streets have not heard
What have we heard
that the streets have not witnessed

Old houses have convoluted memories
New blocks have peculiar expressions

The shadow that a stranger casts on one
in an empty street
The sound that the wind makes
in a secluded corner

What fears that weighed upon our ancestors
in the jungles, beneath the rocks
have the streets not borne

The Full Moon

In the wire cage she dances
several definitions of dance
She has very little on
either her body or her mind
There are beholders whose eyes are full
Their hands reach into their pockets

From the ceiling speakers blast
rhythm bolts upon a smoky crowd
Outside there is silence
Beyond the silence there are wolves
who gaze crazily into the moon

She has a daughter named Cigarette
To have this baby she gave up smoking
The bartender has scars on his face
In the audience a physics professor
writes up his lecture notes
There are hands large and hairy
They run to her like hounds

Through the Window

He should be singing softly
in the rustling of gingko leaves
He should be wearing white
And a white elephant beside him

On the ninth floor of the tower
the air is thin
I wait for my hair
to grow long enough

Something happens to my blood
I can smell the music
An invisible hand takes me
through the labyrinth of light

I am ascending
an ebony palace
The stars settle gently upon my cloak

The Masks

There are masks that are thick and solid
There are masks that are thin and invisible
There are masks that are just make-up

Under palm trees
above the patient sand
life unfolds as a game

If a rock falls from the sky
we can consult either the scientists
or the astrologers
for an explanation
We can also just ignore it
or have it placed in the vegetable garden

It is either a game or a struggle
One can try different masks
This has been said many times

Watching the Sea

A ship sails toward the horizon
its mast lingering
merging with clouds
that bloom into iridescent shapes

It is so obvious
that the Earth is round

You are watching the sea
If you consider yourself beautiful
you fancy someone watching you
Or you imagine someone watching the sea
who can decorate your dreams

It is no coincidence
that the gods resemble us

Dreaming of Light

A white horse comes to you and gently
rubs its nose against your forehead

You mount it
It flies into the ebony night

Stars grow dim and extinguish
revealing dark ribs
of the Universe

You cling to the white horse
It turns and you see
a river of diamonds
spill from Hera's breasts

You ride the white horse through
streets of Darkness
Someone with magnetic breath
tries to suck you in

In the ebony night you cling to Light
It gallops
its hooves triggering soft flames

Passage to Light

A flute calls with languor
It is approaching very slowly

The pale hand of the beloved
A silent monument on an alien planet
The finally irresistible

You have made passage
through swamps and jungles
Here you breathe at ease
and your breath takes you
upon the ladder
of music

VIII

Once in a Train

Once in a Train

A leopard of pure black skin
looked at me intently
A delicate wildness in his clear eyes

A rush of violets

Then he looked away
In the corridor with blowing white curtains
I leaned on the window-sill
Leafless trees and abandoned villages
sped through me

Something gently brushed against my elbow
I knew it was him without looking
Tears made rivers on my face
The wind was tangled by my breath

When I turned around he was gone

On my white arms I saw black
smudges from the window-sill
Drunken men were singing from some compartment
The sleek pale woman in my compartment
lit a cigarette and examined me
from corners of her gray eyes
asked me about my life

She had played cards with him

I lied to her and went back to the corridor
The train seemed to have slowed down
Scattered lights steepened the darkness
It cut into my skin with minute teeth
Within me a cold flood rose
with a lover's silken touch

I could not remember my destination

April, White Blossoms

Across the ocean an old city enters grim rain season
in remembrance of the dead.
My friend's wife wears red rain boots
in a crazed crowd, trying to buy fresh water cress.

I used to examine my own shadow at length, and think
of the ocean.

* * *

If I did not expect eternal love of some ocean,
I would have stayed in the spring of Beijing.
I flew a kite over the Square,
my purple veil blowing in sandy wind.

He loved me once. His wife might have dreamed of me.

* * *

In April the ancient travelers used to pine with broken hearts.
They would seek a shepherd boy
who would point out a small wine village
in profusion of white blossoms.

My friend was out in the streets. His wife was pregnant. I prayed.

I could have been in the crowd, blood stirred by vocal thunders.
I could have lost consciousness in abruptness of a pang
after reflecting in a flash: it might be a rubber bullet.

On the wreaths for the dead, the blossoms are made of
white paper.

Without Fear

I have mounted my throne
in your lap. The river hums
a song of drooping willows and fallen branches.

What is the thin line between instinct and faith

The black dog with neck ribboned in red
jumps for us, its owner watches from a distance.
A plain middle-aged woman.
Across the river two people are fishing.
Here and there tiny flowers in white and purple
and mushrooms shaped like corn-cobs.

What is the thin line between imagination and truth

Down the shore a man in beret
has been wiping his nose most vigorously.
He is very very old.

Attraction

The sky is tiled with dark jade
beneath the fleeting veil of light

We ascend the volcano
to observe the nests of light

All galaxies are dancers in the field
of gravity the universal attraction

We can immortalize each galaxy
A print of light into electricity

The black jade horizon recedes from us

For Rob Kennicutt

Destination

I cradle my daughter in my arms
through miles of rocky path.
A murmur of green in plain gray
sand, along a wild sea.

Let us turn back, my mother says,
This must be it, we have seen it.
Her back has bent for thirty-three years
since the Red Guards forced her
to turn in my father's diaries.

Imperceptibly, the tint intensifies.
Suddenly a green sand beach
nestled beneath black cliffs.

I watch my daughter's fingers
sorting and sieving green gems.
Her tiny braids point up in the wind.
My mother watches me, her thin wrist
holding up her time-invaded face.

Ground into fine jade grains
the song of the secret mountain.
Only the dolphins know.

IX

The Book of Tian

Chapter 1

Prelude

A woman sheds her clothes
a flower blooms

A rose sheds its clothes
the flower vanishes

A woman can not stop weeping
beneath the full moon
All roses have shed their clothes
A gray hair needles through
the dark waterfall of her hair

The wind wraps her in summer arms
The ladder to the sky hangs midair
She can see its end
It is time for a miracle
The temple of Life beckons
with pillared hall and empty altar

Morning Song

You drum with your little feet
against the flesh and skin wall.

Soon, you will emerge
from the long night of waiting
into the sun:
a rush of green banners
against the azure sky,
clouds, flock of white porpoises.

Between sun and sun there will be darkness.
A mountainous cat hides the sky
with its fine, black fur.
The stars will appear to you.
A thousand thoughts will swim into you.

When it rains you will remember
sound of scarlet rivers rushing to the womb.
You will tap your little feet
watching shining rocks after rain.

Recognition

Almost blue almost green
fireflies
drift in the well formed by trees

The sky dizzy with stars
inverted
the stars set free to roam

The infant opens her eyes
round and glowing
Slowly emerging from darkness
Mother's face

Chapter 2

Midnight

If they were to die
she wishes it would be sudden
and painless for her baby

She wishes it would occur
while her baby sucks on her breast
The flow of sweet milk would continue
while they both drift into oblivion

The baby on her breast

Even the thoughts of rotting flesh and maggots
no longer fill her with horrible dread
Her bones would clutch the little baby's
The rest of them would merge
to nourish other life
They would become a new entity
One again at last

Chance

A tiny imperfection magnified
into a world with rainbows and icicles.
A world with perfect precision
would contain nothing.

An invisible, suitable flaw
can propagate
weave into the fabric
a magnificent, absolutely new pattern.

The Boats

The boat brought her the Child.
An ordinary looking boat.
Buddha sat in it crossed legged,
behind him an enormous fan
bearing ancient Chinese inscriptions.
She recognized the calligraphy:
the dancing brush of Su Dong-Po,
another poet obsessed with boats.

Beneath the emerald stars of Egypt
dead Pharaohs waited
for sandalwood boats to ferry them
to the sky and back to life.
Beneath the gold stars of China
poor peasants burned paper boats
to carry their ancestors
across the boundless sea of bitterness.

She shuddered and woke,
walked over to the bassinet to smell the baby.
Any thought, any dream
is a corridor with two open ends,
one inevitably leads to the other.

Chapter 3

Reading People

Some books hide auroras in them
Others vipers and dead bodies
Never close a book that hints at the existence of caverns

Night Song

You came to me in a dream
years before you were conceived
You sat by a stream
held out a little hand to me
Behind you a moist tree
laden with iridescent blossoms

When you squeezed through my insides
I thought I would die of pain
You emerged crying bloody murder
but stopped when I held you
You opened your eyes and gave me a look
I recognized you
You are the one I would give my life for

You are the part of me that I have set free
so that I can hold the Sky in my arms

Imagination

In the bottomless darkness
stars swim at leisure
through the engulfing emptiness.
On each little planet
a new sunrise lights up each dawn.

My Child, be free to not know.

When you are afraid,
imagine yourself naked
curled up like in Mother's womb
falling freely, blissfully
against the dark backdrop of stars.

Notes

1. Li Bai (701–762), whose name has been misspelled historically as "Li Po," is perhaps the most celebrated Chinese poet of all times.

2. Two of the poems in this book, "According to a Leading Cosmologist" and "There Is No Escape," are based on a theoretical astrophysics seminar given by Andrei Linde at Fermi National Accelerator Laboratory.

3. "Tian" means "sky" in Chinese.

4. The Chinese character "jade" is a digitized version of a character written by the Tang dynasty painter Tang Yin.